THE

BOLD

FACTOR

Goal Setting to Ignite Your Life

and Get What You Want!

DEIDRE HUGHEY

Jasten Publishing

Published by Jasten Publishing, Apex, North Carolina
www.jastenpublishing.com

Printed in the United States of America

Library of Congress Cataloging-in-Publication Data has been applied for.

ISBN-13 978-0982719022
ISBN-10 0982719027

FIRST PAPERBACK EDITION

SPECIAL DISCOUNTS ARE AVAILABLE TO YOUR COMPANY, EDUCATIONAL INSTITUTION OR ASSOCIATION
for selling, education purposes, subscription incentives,
gifts or fundraising campaigns.

For more information, please contact the publisher at
Jasten Publishing, Apex, North Carolina
sales@jastenpublishing.com

Dedications

To my dear, understanding husband, Shawn, who has stayed by my side and supported me during my BOLD adventures.

To my wonderful two boys, Steven and Jacob, keep chasing your BOLD dreams every day and don't let anything stop you!

To my dearest friends, Rubye and Karen, thank you for helping me to keep my head above water, for your large shoulders, loving hearts and helping me to "keep it real".

And last, but certainly not least, a humble thanks to God who has shown me grace, mercy and love.

I couldn't have done this without any of you!

Be BOLD!!

NOTE TO READERS

This book is a compilation of information gathered from personal experience as well as hundreds of interviews conducted in person and over the phone while producing and hosting the radio talk show "3 Steps Forward".

While many of my clients have experienced great success in utilizing the strategies outlined in this book, there is no guarantee that these same strategies will work as well for you. These ideas could work better, worse or not at all for you and your given circumstances.

This book is sold with the understanding that neither the author nor the publisher is engaged in rendering legal, financial, accounting, or other professional advice or services. The reader should consult a competent professional before adopting any of the suggestions in this book or drawing inferences from it.

No warranty is made with respect to the accuracy or completeness of the information or referenced contained herein, and both the authors and the publisher specifically disclaim any responsibility for any liability, loss or risk, personal or otherwise, which is incurred as a consequence, directly or indirectly, of the use and application of any of the contents of this book.

In addition, if you experience success from utilizing the enclosed strategies and ideas, neither the author nor the publisher can hold any claim on your benefit, financial or otherwise.

Yep. ;-)

CONTENTS

Introduction i

SMART Goals: What Are They and What's Wrong? 1

Before the BOLD Factor Can Work 17

Big, Bodacious and Ballsy 29

Own Your Outcomes 39

Legendary Love 49

Deliberate Decisions & Determined Actions 57

Where the Rubber Meets the Road 71

Epilogue: Keys to Living a BOLD Life 81

Additional Quotes: 95

About the Author 101

Introduction

"All successful people men and women are big dreamers. They imagine what their future could be, ideal in every respect, and then they work every day toward their distant vision, that goal or purpose."
-Brian Tracy

Success is something that most people want to achieve. Certainly, you're one of those people because you picked up this book.

But, I'm sure you've noticed that sometimes, success seems elusive. Why do some people achieve success while others toil and toil and still only manage to live paycheck to paycheck?

This is a question that drove the outline for my radio show, 3 Steps Forward, and is an overriding premise in every interview I conduct with successful people.

Time and time again, each and every person tells me the same thing - they had to be bold and daring when every rational thought was telling them to stop.

So, how were they able to get past "stop"?

Every person told me that they had a goal in mind, a goal so big that you might categorize their goal as a dream. But to them, their goal was real and their desire was so strong that they weren't willing to let anything stop them, even the voice in their head!

Given this information, it would stand to reason that to become truly successful, you need imagination and boldness in both your personal and business goal setting.

> *"The man who has no imagination has no wings."*
> **Muhammad Ali**

That's exactly what **The BOLD Factor** is about. It's a new way of setting goals and assuring that you reach them!

As you've just read, this is not a new concept. In fact, this methodology, in one form or another has been utilized by countless successful people in history, from explorers to inventors to the greatest business moguls.

So why haven't you heard about **The BOLD Factor** before now?

Well, before now, it really hasn't had a name.

DEFINING THE BOLD FACTOR

I first became interested in this topic as I became successful myself. You see, as I got closer and closer to how I defined success, in many other people's minds, I had already become successful. And, as people perceived my success, they began asking me questions about what my "secret" was.

Over time, I noticed that I was hearing three of the

same questions more frequently than any others.

The 3 Questions

The first two, I typically hear from people that I don't know very well:

1. I don't get it. You're married have two kids and a business. How do you get it all done?

2. How do you know what to do to get successful?

The third one comes after someone knows more about my personal history:

3. How in the world did you get to where you are now after all you've been through?

The Reasons Behind the Questions

Sometimes the reason someone asks a question is more important than the actual question or even the answer. It goes to our motivation, our perception of others and of ourselves.

I've found that most of the time, these particular questions come when people want what someone else has, and they are hoping that there's a secret sauce or secret formula to follow. They have convinced themselves that there's a secret that they haven't stumbled across and they obviously can't be successful unless they have the secret sauce.

The Secret Sauce

There is no secret sauce. Sorry. In fact, there's no secret word, no secret website, no secret formula, no "secret

secret"…

There is, however, action. But action alone won't do it. You have to have a goal to go after: a goal that excites you, a goal that gets you closer to your dreams, a goal that challenges you and makes you feel alive!

And that's where **The BOLD Factor** comes into play.

But, before we get to that…

Answers to the Questions

For those of you that want to know:

1. *I don't get it. You're married have two kids and a business. How do you get it all done?*
   In its simplest terms, I have a plan and I put it into action. The highest priorities in my life are my marriage and my family. I make every effort to ensure that the needs of my family are taken care of and, most importantly, that they feel loved and appreciated. With this in place, I am able to focus on the needs of my business without feeling guilty about ignoring my family during a business deadline.

2. *How do you know what to do to become successful?*
   First, I believe that the quickest way to success is to include other people. Read about people's successes, surround yourself with successful people and ask questions…lots of questions. Limit your time around naysayers and always keep moving forward. Personally, I set my sights on

what I want, find people that have already accomplished that, hire a mentor or coach, put a plan in place, analyze progress and make changes on a regular basis.

3. *How in the world did you get to where you are now after all you've been through?*
   I didn't and still don't listen to small thinkers. In the past, I had people tell me that I would never be successful. I was told that my past would limit my future and potential. What do they know? I say, make peace with your past and create your future!

Now that those are answered, let's take a look at how The BOLD Factor came to be.

Stumbling Blocks to The BOLD Factor

I had made some pretty big goals early in my life and achieved quite a few of them along the way. In my mid-twenties, I got a job working at a corporate giant and learned about SMART goals.

Now, when I first heard about SMART goals, I thought, "This is an awesome idea! This is EXACTLY how goals should be done. It's so logical!!"

When I left my corporate job, I kept utilizing SMART goals, because, well, they make sense! And after all, everyone teaches them: sales trainers, coaches, personal development specialists, etc.

Introduction

In my late 30's I hit a slump and it was almost impossible to get any goals accomplished or to even get excited about my goals. It felt like drudgery.

> *"If everyone is thinking alike, then somebody isn't thinking."*
> **George S. Patton**

I started thinking about how I had accomplished so much when I was in my twenties. As I began to list my successes, I was stunned with the number and the magnitude of them.

Yet, here I was, less than a decade later, barely able to make it through a week of working through a goal before feeling overwhelmed and giving up on achieving it all together.

I wanted to blame it on my age or hormones or just about anything, but I knew that it had to be something else. And, it was important for me to figure it out if I wanted to keep moving forward in my life.

The first thing I did was look at the type of goals that I had in my twenties. When I did, I realized that based on my current SMART goal mindset, I would never have set those goals. Why? Because they were crazy, seemingly unrealistic, daring goals!

This intrigued me because the SMART goals I was making were, well, smart! They were logical, possible and had a set path with an end date. Everyone says that they work!

I realized that there was something that I was missing. Because I'm analytical in nature, I thought it would be interesting and helpful to study how other successful people achieved so many incredible things in their life.

With this in mind, I produced and hosted a radio show for two years, interviewed over 100 people. Each guest was asked to give three actionable steps to help my audience move forward in their lives. Off of the air, I asked many of them about their own successes and how they thought they were able to achieve so much.

During this same time, I also wrote my first book, "I AM Bound and Determined". To create this book, I interviewed 25 women who think of themselves as successful (some are millionaires, gifted entrepreneurs, therapists, etc.) but had experienced trauma in their childhood. I asked each of them why they were able to overcome the odds stacked against them.

I put all of this researched information together, tested the theories and watched as more and more people were able to achieve success with the concepts in the book that you are holding in your hands right now.

I know that the concepts described in **The BOLD Factor** will open your life to greater results and a more exciting, motivating way to take action.

The BOLD Factor will help you to get to where you want to go!

SMART Goals: What Are They and What's Wrong?

Uncovering why we use SMART goals: when it makes sense to use them and when not to.

Don't limit your future by what you understand today. Expand it to what is beyond your belief... it just may happen!

Deidre Hughey

What's Wrong With SMART Goals?

You and I live in an age when we have more information at our fingertips than any other time in history. You can look ANYTHING up!

You can drive down the road, see a sign for a restaurant and look up the reviews before you decide to pull in. You can leave the doctor's office and look up your diagnosis before you leave the parking lot. With just a few keystrokes, you can see the pictures your friends just posted on their Google+ account, Facebook or Twitter.

Google, combined with Smart phones, has made it so that you can find the answer to anything with precision at a moment's notice.

So, if there's so much information at your fingertips, why aren't you wildly successful?

I mean…

> *Don't you already have everything you need?*

Sure you do. You know the drill:

Get an objective in mind.

Then, fit it into the SMART Goal model:[1]

---

[1] November 1981 issue of Management Review by George T. Doran. Doran, G.T. (1981). There's a S.M.A.R.T. way to write management's goals and objectives. Management Review, Volume 70, Issue 11 (AMA FORUM), pp. 35-36

(S) Specific:

Specific refers to making sure the goal is clear. The goal should answer the 5 "w" questions:

> **What:** What do you want to accomplish?

> **Why:** Specific reasons, purpose or benefits of accomplishing the goal

> **Who:** Who is involved?

> **Where:** Identify a location

> **Which:** Identify requirements and constraints

(M) Measurable:

What is going to be the method by which you will measure the progress of accomplishing your goal? In addition, how will you know when the goal has been accomplished?

(A) Attainable:

Make sure that the goal is not out of reach – typically, when a goal is "attainable", you should easily be able to answer the question, "How will the goal be accomplished?"

(R) Relevant:

A relevant goal will be able to answer "Yes" to the following questions:

> Does this goal seem worthwhile?

Is this the right time to go after this goal?

Does the goal match with your other efforts and/needs?

Are you the right person to accomplish the goal?

(T) Timebound
Give your goal a target date for completion – the date should add a sense of urgency, but not so urgent as to counteract any of the aforementioned acronyms

Okay, I don't know about you, but when I read that last section describing SMART goals, my eyes started glazing over by the time I got to the word "Measurable" and I skipped the rest of that section.

And with good reason.

It's BORING!

It does NOTHING to stretch your imagination which is critical in helping you to feel excited and awaken the drive to succeed within your mind!

"People who lean on logic and philosophy and rational exposition end by starving the best part of the mind."
William Butler Yeats

Who Invented SMART Goals?

There is some disagreement to the following assertion, but after spending several hours researching in several different locations for my data, I found that most resources pointed to the following information:

The concept of SMART Goals was created by George Doran. If you're like me, you've never heard of him. In fact, as many times as I've created and utilized SMART goals in my career, I had no idea that he created the format for them prior to researching for this book.

In the November 1981 issue of Management Review, George T. Doran wrote an article in which he described SMART Goals. It would appear that George's objective was to create a basic formula for managers to create goals for themselves, their teams and to teach their teams how to create goals that could then be presented to management.

SMART Goals Inside of Corporate America

For the first time in history, corporations across America had a formula for goals that was logical, detailed and controllable. It was revolutionary! Managers could leave one corporate job, go to another and know that they created and managed goals the same way.

Perfect! And, in fact, it is perfect for a corporation.

Consider this, a manager has a team of 10 individuals and is reasonable for a predefined amount of production from the team. With SMART goals, the manager can lay out goals for each member knowing that each individual team member's goal is Specific, Measurable, Attainable, Relevant and Timebound.

Based on the SMART goal formula, an individual's goal cannot be given to them if it doesn't fit the parameters.

This does two things:
1) It gives a sense of security to the employee who now knows exactly what is expected for the goal to be achieved
2) SMART goals gives the manager and corporation a solid basis for both reward and punishment.

Corporations now had a way to manage the massive numbers of people within its walls and ensure that goals are being set and accomplished in a timely manner. SMART goals made that a reality.

SMART Goals Outside of Corporate America

I bet that George was shocked when he saw SMART goals swoop across the infrastructure of America. I bet he was even more surprised to watch as they began to be taught outside of the confines of corporations.

Why do I think he was surprised? Because I don't believe it's what he intended to have happen. And, I bet he would be the first to tell you that SMART goals don't work in all situations. In fact, if you look at any notable accomplishment in history, you would be hard pressed to back-engineer it into a SMART goal formula.

Actually, let's go this route. Let's try to put a couple of notable accomplishments into the SMART formula.

EXAMPLE #1: Invention of the light bulb

Fit it into the SMART model:

> **Specific – make sure the goal is clear** – the goal should answer the 5 "w" questions
>
> **What: What do you want to accomplish?** Invent the light bulb for home use
>
> **Why: Specific reasons, purpose or benefits of accomplishing the goal** – it would be good to stop using so many candlesticks after the sun goes down
>
> **Who: Who is involved?** Me and whoever I can trust to help out
>
> **Where: Identify a location** – in the workshop
>
> **Which: Identify requirements and constraints –** while every scientific experiments have requirements and constraints, I would wager that some of the constraints were financially bound and others were bound by lack of knowledge or precisely how to invent a light bulb

Measurable – what is going to be the method by which you will measure the progress of accomplishing your goal? Trial and error - **In addition, how will you know**

when the goal has been accomplished? When I have created the light bulb

Attainable – make sure that the goal is not out of reach – typically, when a goal is "attainable", you should easily be able to answer the question, "How will the goal be accomplished?" – I have no idea how I'm going to accomplish this and many people think that my goal is ridiculous - FAIL

Relevant – a relevant goal will be able to answer "Yes" to the following questions:

> **Does this goal seem worthwhile?** YES, well, it does to me

> **Is this the right time to go after this goal?** not sure, but it feels like the right time to me, besides pretty tired of reading by candlelight - FAIL

> **Does the goal match with your other efforts and/or needs?** Not necessarily, could in fact go broke in the pursuit of this goal - FAIL

> **Are you the right person to accomplish the goal?** I think so, but not entirely sure - FAIL

Timebound – give your goal a target date for completion – the date should add a sense of urgency, but not so urgent as to counteract any of the aforementioned acronyms – will accomplish when it's accomplished, will work tirelessly towards the goal until accomplished - FAIL

END of EXAMPLE #1

As you can see, if Thomas Edison[2] had tried to create the light bulb using the SMART goal formula, it wouldn't have been invented. It **couldn't** have been invented because it defies the logical thinking of the SMART formula.

Let's try one that a little more recent…how about the creation of Disneyland?

EXAMPLE #2: Creation of Disneyland

Fit it into the SMART model:

> **Specific – make sure the goal is clear** – the goal should answer the 5 "w" questions
>
> > **What: What do you want to accomplish?** A massive attraction playground for children and adults alike
> >
> > **Why: Specific reasons, purpose or benefits of accomplishing the goal** – there's nothing else like it and it would be fun for families and a challenge for me
> >
> > **Who: Who is involved?** Me and whoever will help out

---

[2] For the intellectuals reading this book, yes, I know that Thomas Edison did not create the first light bulb, but he has been credited with perfecting it for home use. So for the purposes of this book, we'll leave it at that.

> **Where: Identify a location** – Anaheim, outside of Los Angeles
>
> **Which: Identify requirements and constraints** –well, since it's never been done before, can't really say, I suppose financial, people thinking I'm crazy are both constraints - FAIL

Measurable – what is going to be the method by which you will measure the progress of accomplishing your goal? Trial and error - **In addition, how will you know when the goal has been accomplished?** When the park is built and people come and enjoy it

Attainable – make sure that the goal is not out of reach – typically, when a goal is "attainable", you should easily be able to answer the question, "How will the goal be accomplished?" – it's never been done before, and most people think I'm crazy, that it's not possible - FAIL

Relevant – a relevant goal will be able to answer "Yes" to the following questions:

> **Does this goal seem worthwhile?** YES…to me
>
> **Is this the right time to go after this goal?** I have no idea, just feels right - FAIL

Does the goal match with your other efforts and/or needs? Not necessarily, could in fact go broke in the pursuit of this goal and risk my credibility - FAIL

Are you the right person to accomplish the goal? I believe that I am...if not me, who will?

Timebound – give your goal a target date for completion – the date should add a sense of urgency, but not so urgent as to counteract any of the aforementioned acronyms – will accomplish when it's accomplished, will work tirelessly towards the goal until accomplished or run out of money - FAIL

END of EXAMPLE #2

You may notice that the two examples above have many of the same fail points within the SMART methodology of goal setting.

The good news: SMART goals were created as a methodology for helping management of corporations to be able to track goals and the accomplishment of goals within their teams.

The bad news: SMART goals stifle the creativity and imagination of those that use them limiting successes to the constraints of what is considered attainable.

The BOLD News: You don't have to use SMART goals!

The SMART Goals Conclusion

I've read hundreds of books on personal development, business success, motivation, and inspiration. I love watching A&E specials on the successes of inventors, business greats and our country's growth. I've listened to hundreds of hours of interviews on mp3's about how people attain success. And, I have spent over 3 years interviewing growth experts, business successes and marketing moguls.

After you fill your senses with enough information and begin to disseminate it, you begin to notice patterns. The biggest pattern that I noticed was the lack of mention of SMART goals in the conversations.

This intrigued me.

I then analyzed how I've been able to accomplish what I have (considering my crazy background, which you can read about in the "About the Author" section of this book) and came up with my own formula. I then took that formula and compared it to the stories that I had read and the interviews that I had participated in.

Yes, you know where this is going. The **BOLD Factor** fit!

> *"I took the road less traveled by
> and that has made all the difference."*
> **Robert Frost**

The creation of and the aspiration of **BOLD** goals are not for the faint of heart. In fact, **BOLD** goals will challenge you and change you. If you're happy with who you are right now and have no desire for exponential growth, **BOLD** goals are NOT for you.

However, if you're ready to eliminate your obstacles and achieve any goal that you set for yourself, **The BOLD Factor** is exactly what you have been looking for!

Just think…

what goal would you go after?

how would your life change?

what would it feel like?

how would your business change?

Have you thought about it? Are your creative juices starting to flow?

~~~

BOLD Factor Reflections:

Can you think of any other accomplishments in history that would not fit into the SMART model of goal setting?

Are there any goals that you have thought about going after in the past and struggled putting into the SMART goal framework?

Are you truly open to learning about a new way of goal setting and achievement?

Before the BOLD Factor Can Work

Ahhh, pre-work…

As much as you might want to skip this

DON'T

"A woman who is convinced that she deserves to accept only the best challenges herself to give the best. Then she is living phenomenally."

Maya Angelou

Before the BOLD Factor Can Work

This chapter is all about helping you to release your mind from the constraints of mediocrity and the gray, bleak world of conformity.

Your Powerful Brain:

Your mind is a tricky thing…it's incredibly adaptable and able to take on incredible tasks. Your mind can think quickly and evoke incredible emotions and senses throughout your body.

Another amazing aspect of your mind is that it can also ignore routine noises, once you accept that the noises aren't a danger to you. This is why people can live in the flight path of airplanes or next to train tracks, and in a very short period of time, they aren't able to "hear" the airplanes or trains.

However, this concept actually leads into what I call "lazy brain". You see, your mind would actually prefer not to work hard. This is one of the reasons it ignores the airplane or train noise. It's also why habits are so powerful. Think about it. A habit is created through repetition. This repetition becomes so entrenched in your brain that is can actually put itself on autopilot. In some respects, habits create an even lazier brain. Good news for a good habit, bad news for one that you don't want.

Your Lazy Brain:

I have found with myself, clients and the hundreds of interviews that I've conducted that we all struggle with "lazy brain".

You see, while you may work hard to create a habit that you want, your mind is continually trying to create habits that you may or may not desire. It's attempting to create habits that enable it to be, well, lazy.

These lazy habits rob you of joy and awareness. Before you know it, you find yourself bored on a regular basis. Life seems less exciting and much more mundane. You feel generally less happy and less fulfilled.

This is because, even though your brain enjoys being lazy, the core of who you are, does not enjoy it at all. It doesn't matter whether you refer to this part of yourself as your core, your spirit, your energy, your soul or anything else, trust me, it craves excitement, exhilaration and challenge!

Your Core vs. Your Brain:

Unfortunately for most of you, and on a daily basis, these two diametrically opposed forces fight their battle for superiority in secret. And, do you want to take a guess as to which one wins? Yep, you guessed it, your brain.

And every time your brain wins, it squashes the hope that your core has for excitement, exhilaration and challenge. This is what you need to be aware of. This is what you have to fight. In fact, this is where some of your fears come from.

Think about it. Have you ever thought about doing something exciting (jumping out of an airplane, bungee jumping, rock climbing, producing videos, becoming an entrepreneur, etc.) but the more you think about it, the more reasons you come up with to not do it? In fact, the more you think about it, the more dangers and fears you can express about going through with it! This is your brain courageously fighting to stay lazy.

Fortunately, there is a solution! You can use the same tactics that your brain uses to stay lazy to help it come into alignment with your core.

Step #1: Let's first take a look at what brings you joy.

Take a moment and list 50 things that make you happy. If your imagination has been constrained, you may be rolling your eyes at me right now. 50 things? Yes, 50 things. These can be people, places, events, memories…they can be things that you haven't seen in a long time, thoughts of things you would like to do.

For those of you that are truly having extreme difficulty and need some inspiration, you can go to my website and download a resource that will give you some inspiration to help you.

Simply go to:
www.deidrehughey.com/BOLDFactorResources
and download the **Joy List Resource**.

~~~

Once you've completed this first step, wipe your brow, pat yourself on the back and start the second step.

Everything that is new or uncommon raises a pleasure in the imagination, because it fills the soul with an agreeable surprise, gratifies its curiosity, and gives it an idea of which it was not before possessed.
Joseph Addison

Step #2: What's on your bucket list?

If you already have a bucket list, take it out and go over it. Refresh it with new ideas and cross out items you've already accomplished or don't interest you anymore.

If you don't have a bucket list, then today you're going to start one!

Make a list of 50 things that you would like to do, see or accomplish before you die. Again, this will be difficult for some of you and a breeze for others.

I've created a resource to help you with this task. You can go to my website and download the **Bucket List Resource**.

Simply go to:
www.deidrehughey.com/BOLDFactorResources
and download the **Bucket List Resource**.

Step #3: What do you wish was different about who you are? OR, what are your worst qualities?

We all wish that there were things that were different about ourselves. We wish we weren't as fat, skinny, lazy, ADHD, short, tall, blond, brunette, scared, fearless, finicky, caring, boring, zealous, etc.

Because of that, this will probably be the easiest list for you to write. And precisely why you are limited to writing 10 things. That's it.

I'm limiting you to 10 things because part of making **BOLD** decisions, breakthroughs and utilizing **The BOLD Factor** means that you will have to think more powerfully and positively rather than negatively.

I want to take a moment here and talk with you about how you view yourself and negative thinking in general.

Negative thinking is crippling to achieving more in your life. It can stop you from achieving your goals or even creating them in the first place. The most crippling of all negative thinking are the negative thoughts that we have about ourselves.

How You See Yourself

With my personal clients, I have them write out this list and I review it with them. Then I have them mark the items that they can change about themselves with an asterisk. For every item listed that is something they can't change, I have them go back and rewrite it into a positive statement.

For example, Susie writes that one of the things she wishes was different about her is that she wishes she wasn't so tall (6′ 2″). She rewrote it into a statement that said, "My height means that I can easily dunk a basketball, got a basketball scholarship for college, my kids friends think I'm amazing and oh, I NEVER have problems getting things off of the top shelf."

You see, because she was focusing on the negative (not being a "normal" height) she wasn't allowing herself to see the positive things that have happened in her life as a result.

For the other items on the list, the ones that you can change, I verify with my clients the veracity of their claim and then ask them to take the list to a couple of their closest friends. When they return to me, there are always interesting results.

The most common is that their friends see them MUCH differently than they see themselves and almost always MUCH more positively than they've made themselves out to be.

I challenge you to do the same. Write your list, separate them into things you can and can't change. Rewrite the items that you can't change into positive statements and bring the rest of your list to your friends and get their feedback.

So, go ahead, write a list of 10 things that you wish was different about you.

> *Your life is your message. What is it saying?*
> **Deidre Hughey**

Step #4: What are your best characteristics? What do you like most about yourself?

For this list, you need to write a list of 30 things.

STOP the moaning and groaning.

Trust me, there are at least 30 things that are awesome about who you are, your character and personality. They can be about how you think, how you feel, what you believe, what you value…anything that you feel deserves your praise…deserves high regard for who you are. Write it all down.

Then read it again.

It may be your favorite thing to read for weeks to come.

I've created another resource that could help you called the **Awesome Character Resource**.

Simply go to:
www.deidrehughey.com/BOLDFactorResources
and download the **Awesome Character Resource**.

And, onward to the final step of your pre-work…

Step #5: What are you willing to give up?

Huh? Yeah, here's the thing about success. You ALWAYS have to give something up. It may be sleep, arrogance, comfort, self-righteousness or anyone of the "deadly sins": wrath, greed, sloth, pride, lust, envy or gluttony. Success costs.

Let's say that you weigh 250 pounds and you decide that you want to get in shape and get to a size 8. Chances are you are going to have to exercise (give up laziness), get up early to exercise before work (give up sleep), follow an exercise routine (give up comfort), maybe buy some workout clothes (give up money), buy more clothes as you lose weight (give up money), follow a new diet program (giving up comfort, money and your favorite foods), ask for help when you plateau (give up pride), etc…

There are always things that you will not give up and it's good to know what those are before you make a commitment. I know that for myself, I'm not willing to do anything that would compromise my relationship with my husband or with my children. Maybe time with your family is really important to you too.

But there are many other factors to consider: maybe you're not willing to wake up early, give up your daily television shows or your favorite dessert!

Now that you have a few examples, let's talk about how this works. On a piece of paper, you're going to divide your sheet into 2 columns. The left column will have what you're willing to give up and the right column are the things that you will not give up or compromise.

I've already created this template for you. You can go to my website and download this sheet.

Simply go to:
www.deidrehughey.com/BOLDFactorResources
and download the **Personal Values Resource**.

~~~

BOLD Factor Reflections:

I don't recommend that you move on to the rest of the **BOLD Factor** chapters until you've completed this pre-work. This pre-work is extremely helpful, and you will find it invaluable and necessary to successfully accomplishing your goals. In fact, for the members of my **BOLD Factor Club**, individuals don't have access to the next sections until they have successfully completed the pre-work.

In my online **BOLD Factor Club**, members have access to personal attention from me or a member of my team to help in completing the pre-work, as well as, the help and support of the other members as everyone helps to mentor each other through the process.

This is important as the pre-work will be utilized and referred to as a personal resource for you in making decisions, inspiring you and reminding you of your commitments to yourself.

Please use the resources available to you on my website to complete your reflections for this chapter:
www.deidrehughey.com/BOLDFactorResources

Big, Bodacious and Ballsy

Because nothing, absolutely, positively nothing
is exciting about...

little, tiny goals

Trust that little voice in your head that says "wouldn't it be interesting if…"; And then do it.

Duane Michals

Big, Bodacious and Ballsy

Yes, I said it…you need to make big, bodacious, ballsy goals.

So what does that mean?

Let's take each adjective, one at a time…

BIG:
Of considerable size, extent, or intensity

So, what makes a goal "big"?

First, it blows the doors off of any other goal you've made before. It's something that can't be accomplished in the next 30 days. In fact, it may take the next 1, 5 or 10 years to make your goal become a reality!

I know, this flies in the face of everything you've ever been taught. But, if your goal can be accomplished in the next 30 days, then you are only thinking in terms of stepping stones to your ultimate goal.

Let's take a look at Roger Bannister…the first man to break the 4 minute mile. He accomplished this feat in 1954, over 30 years before the creation of S.M.A.R.T. goals. Yet, this is seen as one of the most pivotal events in the history of sport of running.

What's even more interesting is that his goal of breaking the 4 minute mile was spurred by his participation in the 1952 Olympics. He broke a British record, but it was not enough for a medal as he placed 4th in the race. Roger went home and thought about giving up running altogether.

Then something inside of him drove him to go after a big goal, an unthinkable goal...an impossible goal. Instead of giving up running, Roger Bannister decided that he was going to be the first man to run a mile in less than 4 minutes.

Anything can spur you towards your goal. Whether your catalyst is success, defeat or simply an idea, the most important thing is that it's big.

Because a big goal is worth going after. A big goal will push you and drive your desire to accomplish it.

We're living in a time when the world has suddenly discovered India because it's run out of raw material for its imagination. The raw materials for imagination are inexhaustible here.
Deepak Chopra

BODACIOUS:

1. Excellent, admirable, or attractive

2. Audacious in a way considered admirable

In order for your goal to be bodacious, it has to be something that would be considered admirable not only by you, but by people that would witness your success.

Many times, a bodacious goal seems ridiculous in its undertaking, not simply because the goal is big, but because people believe that it can't be done. However, people would be pleasantly surprised when you do and admire you for it.

Let's use Roger Bannister's goal to break the 4 minute mile. This was a big goal, but the knowledge of how difficult it would be to accomplish made it bodacious. A goal that when it was achieved brought admiration to Roger that still continues to this day even though many people have beat the 4 minute mile since.

What about your goal? Do you admire your goal? Is it excellent? Is it something you can get excited about achieving?

Here's the test to see if your big goal is also bodacious:

When you imagine yourself reaching your big, bodacious goal, it fills you with excitement! You can see the changes in your life that happen as a result of achieving it. People admire you for having achieved your goal because they admire both your goal and the fact that you achieved it. Your self-confidence grows because you did it...you achieved your big, bodacious goal.

Do you see it? Is it exciting to imagine yourself accomplishing it? Can you see how your life would change?

Good! Then you've made your goal big and bodacious!

BALLSY:

Tough and courageous

Are you getting this? Look, a ballsy goal will NOT be easy to accomplish. It will take sacrifice on your part.

A ballsy goal will change you at your core. At times, you will have to reach deep inside of yourself to find the strength to keep moving forward. In fact, you may fail on your way to accomplishing your goal.

Friends and family think that your big, bodacious, ballsy goal is crazy and can't imagine how you're ever going to accomplish it. There are times when you shake your head and wonder if maybe they're right…maybe it's insanity.

But, there's a nagging sense inside of you that is screaming for you to accomplish it! You picture yourself climbing your mountainous goal and the pride that you would feel for yourself, the sense of wonder and amazement that you did it, you pushed yourself through every obstacle.

It was hard, but you saw it through!!

> *You have every right to an amazing life,*
> *go for it!*
> **Deidre Hughey**

A ballsy goal makes the idea of trying to figure out how to accomplish your goal send a shiver of intimidation down your spine and makes little to no sense to most of the people that you tell.

A big goal can't be accomplished quickly and will seem crazy to your friends and family.

A bodacious goal is an attractive, admirable goal.

A ballsy goal will take courage and be tough to complete.

A big, bodacious, ballsy goal is a worthy goal…a goal that is worthy of what you are capable of.

~~~

BOLD Factor Reflections:

Take a moment and on the following pages write down 1-3 big, bodacious and ballsy goals that excite you!

Goal #1: _____

What makes this goal big?

What makes this goal bodacious?

What makes this goal ballsy?

Why is this Big, Bodacious, Ballsy goal exciting to you?

How would your life change if you were to accomplish this goal?

Goal #2: _____

What makes this goal big?

What makes this goal bodacious?

What makes this goal ballsy?

Why is this Big, Bodacious, Ballsy goal exciting to you?

How would your life change if you were to accomplish this goal?

Goal #3: _____

What makes this goal big?

What makes this goal bodacious?

What makes this goal ballsy?

Why is this Big, Bodacious, Ballsy goal exciting to you?

How would your life change if you were to accomplish this goal?

After looking at the goals that you wrote, which one excites you the most?

Own Your Outcomes

Everything you do or don't do has an outcome.

It's the truth.

Own it.

True joy comes from overcoming the things in your life that you once thought were out of reach.

Deidre Hughey

Own Your Outcomes

You may not like this chapter.

This is the chapter where I'm going to kick your butt a little bit. But before I do, I want you to know why I'm doing it. You see, "lazy brain" leads to lazy people, lazy people leads to unhappiness, unhappiness leads to frustration and frustration leads to the inability to achieve goals.

This book is all about how you can achieve the goals that matter most to you, and in order to do that, you have to break the cycle!

So, take a moment to take a personal inventory of yourself. Take a close look at who you are right now...and I mean a really good look. Take a look at yourself physically, mentally, and spiritually – look outside, look inside, look at your character, look at your success... look at everything.

Do you like what you see?

Now, if you like what you see, then that's awesome! You can pat yourself on the back for kicking your own butt along the way, giving yourself some tough love and taking responsibility for your life. In my experience, you're one of the rare top 3% of people in the world. You achieve goals on a regular basis, you've found joy and satisfaction in your life and don't have a problem pushing yourself past your preconceived limits. Congratulations on a job well done!

What about the rest of you? When you stop and take a good look at your life, there are parts that you don't like to see, right?

Well, that's your fault.

Now, I know. You want to tell me all about how you've had a tough break in life, you had a horrible upbringing, your parents beat you and you were raped. Your parents were drug addicts and you can't trust people. You traveled so much growing up that you didn't have time to make friends and it's affected your current relationships. As an adult, you've been divorced 3 times and you're beginning to think you can never have a healthy relationship. And then you…blah, blah, blah…

Join the club.

Now before you start screaming about how insensitive and unfeeling I am, keep reading.

Most of us have had tragic instances in our lives. Some more than others, but it's a rare person that is able to grow up unscathed by the ills of being surrounded by other humans.

Don't get me wrong. I think it's horrific the way some of you have been raised and it sickens me when I think about some of the stories that I've heard.

And trust me, I've heard some doozies. Some of the most tragic stories I've ever heard are in my book, *I AM Bound and Determined: The Must Read Guide for Women of Childhood Abuse and Trauma*. (With integrity, I can honestly recommend this as a "Must Read" if you find that it's difficult for you to let the past go and move forward. There are 25 amazing women waiting to tell you how they did just that and found success in their lives.)

Whatever you can tell me about your life, I've probably heard it before or something like it. In fact, a lot of your stories are my stories. I was neglected by my parents, molested by a neighbor, my uncle, diagnosed with bipolar depression and a borderline personality disorder, suicidal, committed to a psychiatric institution, raped twice, had two abortions and was addicted to drugs.

However, I would wager that most of your stories are in your past. They happened. You can't change it. But you can change who you are now and where you're going.

Who you are now, right now in life, is your responsibility.

But until a person can say deeply and honestly, "I am what I am today because of the choices I made yesterday," that person cannot say, "I choose otherwise."
Stephen R. Covey

It's your fault if you still struggle with things that you blame on your past. And as long as you blame your past, you can't look forward into the future and make a significant difference in your life or the life of others.

It doesn't matter what's happened to you. What matters is who you want to be, where you want to go and what you're willing to do to make your life better. Make your life incredible!

I've interviewed over 100 people with amazing stories of resilience and it never stops amazing me what we're capable of overcoming. My story is not the most tragic I've heard, but for some of you, my past is shocking.

Yet, I've been able to overcome it and move forward.

You can too.

You have the ability to make mountainous changes in your life and overcome tremendous odds if you're ready.

It's never too late to be what you might have been.
George Eliot

And, if this is a sticking point for you, if you're wondering when you'll be ready, I'll let you in on a secret.

Readiness is not a parameter for moving forward. It honestly does not matter if you're ready.

The question is, "When are you going to make the decision to move forward?" And that decision doesn't have to take a long time to work itself out, it can happen in a split second.

Think about it.

When many couples find out that they're pregnant, the first thing they ask themselves is, "Are we really ready for this?"

The answer is, "It doesn't matter – the baby is coming whether you're ready or not!"

Readiness is a decision. Make a decision that you're going to change and you can start changing.

Own it.

Own who you are and then own what happens as a result of your moving forward.

Your outcomes are yours. They are your fault.

It's time to be proud of your outcomes and feel awesome!

That's **The BOLD Factor!**

~~~

If the idea of readiness being a decision is still causing some difficulty or calls into question some of your current beliefs, then please listen to the following interview on my website with Margie Warrell, author of Find Your Courage and Stop Playing Safe. I believe you will find this incredibly beneficial.

Simply go to:
www.deidrehughey.com/BOLDFactorResources
and listen to this fantastic and inspirational interview.

~~~

BOLD Factor Reflections:

Is there any part of you that is struggling with taking full responsibility for where you are right now? If so, what excuses are you using to justify not taking responsibility?

If you answered yes, what can you do today to eliminate those excuses from your life?

Do you believe you're ready to move forward and own some new outcomes in your life?

What outcome or change in your life are you most looking forward to occurring?

Legendary Love

If you won't give yourself a swift kick in the
butt when you need it…who will?

*Can you imagine what you would do if you
would do all you can?*

Sun Tzu

Legendary Love

So, you may be thinking to yourself, "What in the world does love have to do with goal setting?"

Everything.

Remember, we're talking about doing something BOLD, something significant, something that will make a difference in your life and potentially in the people around you.

Why Love a Goal?

Well, it actually has to do with more than just loving your goal, but let's start there.

Loving the Goal:

You have to have enough love, enough passion for what it is that you want to accomplish to see the goal through to the end. And here's why...

If you don't love your goal and truly want to see it happen, you will falter. And actually, I can guarantee you that you will struggle on your path to accomplishing your goal.

Remember the list that you created in the pre-work where you listed all of the types of things that you were willing to give up to accomplish your goal?

Remember the list that you wrote in **Own Your Outcomes**? The one where you wrote out all of the ways your life would change and how you would feel the moment you realized that you had accomplished your goal?

This is one of the reasons that you wrote those.

You see, you have a greater chance of making it happen if you keep in mind an understanding of what accomplishing the goal will do for you and for others.

Love the goal, love what will be and love you!

Loving You:

Yes, you need to love yourself. You have to take care of yourself, appreciate who you are now and how accomplishing this goal will change you.

Understand that you will need to love yourself enough to make difficult decisions, to love yourself enough to push yourself when it looks like you won't ever make your goal, to love yourself and your goal when your friends and family are asking you why you're trying so hard.

At those moments, you will pull on the love that you have for yourself and tell yourself that you believe in yourself and that your goal is worthy.

You may be wondering, "Is that what makes it legendary?"

No.

Legendary Love:

What makes love legendary is when you push yourself through things when everything else in your system says that it's time to quit because you hear yourself saying:

- *it's too hard*

- *maybe I'll never make it*

- *what if my friends are right*

- *maybe I'm just not cut out for this*

- *I just want to be comfortable*

You WILL think those things and you have to tell yourself to quit whining and get moving!

No one is going to come rescue you and no one is going to do it for you. YOU have to do it for you and you won't if you don't love yourself enough to give yourself a swift kick in the butt.

Slap yourself in the face, kick yourself in the butt, put your adult shoes on and get it done!

Challenge yourself today! Facing and overcoming challenges builds confidence and helps you to feel love from yourself and for others.
Deidre Hughey

The ability to push yourself through when everyone else fails only happens when you :

- **don't accept excuses from yourself**

- **believe the giving up is unacceptable**

- **whining and complaining is offensive**

THAT is Legendary Love.

I guarantee you that if you are honest and if you have enough passion for your goal, for yourself and where you want to go, you'll find the strength to practice Legendary Love.

It's not your job to like me – it's mine.
Byron Katie

~~~

BOLD Factor Reflections:

Have you chosen a goal that you love?

Do you struggle with loving yourself? If so, what can you do to change that today?

Do you see how loving yourself and loving your goal(s) are essential to making momentous change for yourself and/or for your business? Specifically, how do you see this helping you?

Deliberate Decisions &
Determined Actions

Are you ready to feel the grit?

Take a bite and relish it...

Determination will get you further than talent.

Stephanie Damore

Deliberate Decisions

As I was getting ready to write this chapter, I sat down and had coffee with a friend. We began discussing the book and she asked me, "So, I just don't get it. What's the difference between deliberate decisions and the decisions I make every day?"

It's true, you make decisions every single day. You decide to do things and you decide not to do things. Sometimes, you even choose not to make a decision (which, by the way, is actually a decision also, just not a very beneficial one).

You may, in fact, make deliberate decisions already, but for most people, this simply isn't true.

Let me explain.

Being deliberate about anything takes thought. First, let's take a look at the definition of the word deliberate.

DELIBERATE:

ADJ: Done consciously and intentionally: "a deliberate attempt to provoke conflict"

VERB: Engage in long and careful consideration: "she deliberated over the menu".

Making deliberate decisions means that they need to be intentional decisions, decisions that are made with thought.

You may be saying, "Now, wait a minute Deidre. The very definition of a decision means that there has to be thought behind it."

I beg to differ.

Low Priority and Begrudged Decisions

There are many instances when we make decisions that aren't necessarily entirely deliberate. Most of these types of decision fall into one of two categories: Low Priority Decisions and Begrudged Decisions.

Low Priority Decisions

Low priority decisions happen with such a high frequency, I would wager that once you read about them, you will be able to point out how these play out in your life on a weekly or even daily basis.

Have you ever been driving home and made the decision to stop at the grocery store along the way. Then as you're pulling into your driveway realized you "forgot" to stop at the grocery store?

You say that you "forgot", I say that you made an unconscious, habitual decision to go home. Stopping at the grocery store wasn't given enough emphasis and therefore, a low priority in your mind.

Let me give you another example.

You've been busy working when you realize that you don't have something you need. For this example, let's say that you need a magic marker. You know that the magic marker is in another room. So, you make the very simple decision to go get it. You leave your work, go to the room where the magic marker is and you "forgot" what you went into the room for.

You say that you "forgot", I say that you weren't completely conscious or present when you made the decision in the first place. Because your mind was filled with other thoughts and decisions that you were making and thinking about, the action to get the marker got a lower and lower priority in your mind.

In fact, the decision to get the marker was at such a low priority in your mind that by the time you got to the room, you couldn't even remember you made the decision in the first place. All you can figure out is that you made a decision to come into the room. And honestly, the only reason you know that is because you can't deny that you're standing in the room looking for something!

Begrudged Decisions

If you have a good sense of who you are, then "begrudged decisions" happen with much less frequency. However, it's still easy to fall into the trap of this type of decision.

A "begrudged decision" is any decision that you make without your full heart, mind and soul behind it. Typically, this type of decision is one that you make at the request or pressure from someone else. While not having your heart, mind and soul behind the decision makes it similar to the "low priority decision", the main difference is that a begrudged decision has the added dimension of pressure or even guilt.

One of my clients was unhappy in her work. Now, from all outside appearances, she seemed to be extremely successful. She had a thriving chiropractic practice with multiple practitioners, yet she suddenly found herself in a position of not being able to attain any of the goals she set for her business.

After talking with her for a while, she revealed that she had never wanted to be a chiropractor, but her father was a chiropractor and was so very proud of her. When I asked what she was passionate about, she told me that she had always wanted to be a teacher and now felt that it was too late. After all of this came out, we were also able to discover that she was in fact, unconsciously sabotaging her own efforts.

Because the decision to become a chiropractor was made begrudgingly, she now found herself in a position of self-sabotage. She now had to find a way to make it her decision and find other outlets for her passion, or to leave her current position and pursue a teaching career.

Begrudged Decisions are not always imposed on you from other people. In fact, you may be doing this to yourself right now as a begrudged decision happens anytime you make a decision that you "should" make.

Ever looked in the mirror and thought, "I should go on a diet," or "I really should be exercising"? Anytime you make a decision because it's something you should do, you are doomed to eventually fail whatever goal you set for yourself based on that decision.

Why?

Because making a decision based on what you "should" do, is a decision based on guilt. Any decision based on feeling guilty will eventually backfire as your spirit or core builds resentment about not being included in the decision making process.

In the end, a deliberate decision is a conscious decision, a decision made with focus and clarity. A deliberate decision cannot be made while you have "other things on your mind" or don't have a buy in from your entire being.

Speaking on not having a "buy in", I think it's important to address another issue that effects whether or not your decisions will be successfully deliberate. Unfortunately, there is a belief that many women have that is in fact, a myth. That myth is that you are an incredible multi-tasker.

The Multi-Tasking Lie

There has been study after study done about multi-tasking and in every single study, it has been found that our brains are not meant to multi-task.

I guarantee that some of you will read that and argue with me. You believe that you are incredible, awe-inspiring multi-taskers and are outside of the confines of these studies.

You're saying, "Well, they haven't studied me!"

True, but studies have been done with people that don't claim to be multi-taskers and people that claim to be chronic multi-taskers. The results are conclusive. If you are a great multi-tasker, you are lying to yourself. I'm not telling you that you can't multi-task, I'm just saying you don't do it as well as you think. It's simply not the way human brains work.

I have two resources on my website if you would like to take a deeper look into this statement. The first is an article that I wrote delving into two of the studies and how to combat multi-tasking and the other is a brief video that I produced. The video will take you through a short demonstration enabling you to experience first-hand how poorly your brain multi-tasks.

Simply go to:
www.deidrehughey.com/BOLDFactorResources
and watch the video entitled, "**Multi-Tasking Takedown**"

Now that you've read this chapter and watched my video, it has to be clear that you cannot make deliberate decisions while multi-tasking. Deliberate decisions must be made when you are focused on the one decision.

Deliberate Decisions and Sacrifice

Sacrifice?

Yes, in order for your decisions to be deliberate, you will need to reflect on your list of "What you would be willing to give up" and understand what sacrifice(s) you willingly offer to ensure that your deliberate decision will have an associated determined action to make it happen.

Think about it. Have you ever taken action before and then stopped before achieving your goals? Chances are, this has happened to you on more than one occasion. And, there may be any number of reasons that you didn't complete your action.

However, more often than not, you didn't take into consideration what you would need to give up in order for your decision to be fulfilled.

Non-Deliberate Decision Example

You go to bed at night thinking about how first thing in the morning, you're going to exercise and eat healthy. You get up and realize that your workout clothes are in the laundry. You think, "No problem, I'll work out when I get home."

You walk downstairs and the coffee cake that you bought just the day before is sitting on the counter. You stop in the hallway and you lean your ear towards the coffee cake...you think it might be calling to you. You think to yourself, "Ooops, I forgot about that. Well, that would simply be a waste of money. I guess I'll just start exercising and eating healthy tomorrow."

This is a perfect example of a decision that wasn't made deliberately. It is almost impossible to make a deliberate decision while your mind is in the middle of winding down for sleep. There was little intention or consideration in the decision making process. If there had been, you would have made the decision before you went to bed, laid out your workout clothes, set your alarm earlier, etc. You would have given careful consideration as to what you would need to give up for the decision to be successful (e.g. sleep, comfort, fatty foods, etc).

Determined Actions

Once you have made a deliberate decision, action will need to take place in order for your decision to become a reality. Fortunately, determined action is much simpler when a deliberate decision has been made. Making deliberate decisions begins to give your mindset momentum towards achievement.

Just think about the previous example. If you had made a deliberate decision, your activities would have looked more like this:

As a part of the deliberate decision making process, you would have been prepared with an understanding of what you were willing to give up. You make a decision that you was willing to give up sleeping in, only eat foods that nourish your body and prepare yourself for success before you go to sleep at night

As a part of the determined action process, you make sure that there are healthy foods in the house, you set out your workout clothes the night before, and set your alarm to wake up early enough in the morning to workout.

The start or preparation phase of the determined action process, which is the easiest part, also makes the harder part of action, the actual workout, easier to make happen as excuses have been stripped away.

Another benefit to making deliberate decisions is that if you think about taking action and begin making excuses (which your "lazy brain" is more than happy to make for you), you have several tools in your arsenal to combat the excuses:

1. **reflect upon your deliberate decision**

2. **remind yourself what that decision is trying to achieve**

3. **remind yourself how you'll feel when you're successful**

4. **remind yourself what you promised yourself that you would sacrifice for that result.**

Then, make the decision to be true to yourself, to be honest with yourself and be proud of your decisions. The moment you follow through, congratulate yourself for following through!!

~~~

BOLD Factor Reflections:

For you, how are deliberate decisions different from the decisions you are used to making?

Are you a recovering multi-tasker? If so, what are you going to do to combat this in your quest towards accomplishing your BOLD goal?

Are you ready to make deliberate decisions and take determined actions to accomplish your BOLD goal(s)?

Where the Rubber Meets the Road

Are You Comfortable?

There's nothing wrong with comfort,
as long as it's momentary.

Face your challenges,
get uncomfortable,
and grow!!

It is not the critic who counts, not the man who points out how the strong man stumbled or where the doer of deeds could have done better. The credit belongs to the man who is actually in the arena, whose face is marred by dust, and sweat, and blood; who strives valiantly, who errs and comes short again and again; who knows the great enthusiasms, the great devotions and spends himself in a worthy cause; who at best knows achievement and who at the worst if he fails, at least fails while doing greatly, so that his place shall never be with those cold and timid souls who know neither victory nor defeat.

Theodore Roosevelt

Where the Rubber Meets the Road

Congratulate yourself! If you've been following the instructions along the way, you now have an incredible BOLD goal:

B – you have a big, bodacious and ballsy goal that excites you!

O - you have taken ownership of where you are right now and you're ready to take ownership of your upcoming outcomes

L – you have a love for your goal, you love yourself and you're ready to be tough with yourself when you start complaining and whining

D – you're ready to make deliberate decisions, you understand the sacrifices that you have to make and you're ready to take determined action to get closer to the success of your goal!

If that is all true for you, pat yourself on the back. If the list looks attractive to you, but this isn't where you are, go back to whatever chapter you need to and get up to speed.

As soon as you are ready, the rest of this chapter is waiting for you to help you put it all together and start making a difference in your life…a difference that will astound you and everyone who watches you go after your goals!

Moving Forward and Staying On Track

So, now you have a BOLD goal. And if you step away and look at it for a moment, looking at your goal may do several things to you and your psyche.

In fact, at various points in time and depending on how you're feeling in any given day, that goal may:

1. fill you with excitement and anticipation at completing such a worthy goal

2. fill you with dread at the prospect of how long it's going to take you to accomplish it

3. fill you with anxiousness and concern at the prospect of how difficult your day to day tasks are going to be in order to accomplish your goal

4. overwhelm you and stop you in your tracks at the very idea of starting to work on such an enormous undertaking

5. fill you with awe when you dream of completing it

Those are all intense and very real feelings! You may on any given day be filled with excitement, anticipation, dread, anxiousness, concern, overwhelm or awe.

So, let's talk about how you are going to use the energy from those feeling to your advantage, rather than having them control and manipulate you into failure.

Now, just because you have a feeling, doesn't mean you need to bow down to that feeling.

The best way that I've found that has worked for me and hundreds of my clients. I call it the 30-Day Reset.

30-Day Reset came about in an effort to keep myself on track.

You see, what I was observing in myself is that when I attempted anything truly worthwhile, many times, I would find myself daunted by the vastness of my undertaking. This thinking and feeling would not happen immediately, but after the excited novelty of what I was setting out to accomplish wore off, all I was left with was the overwhelming understanding of how long the effort was going to take.

Then it came to me, what if I looked at it in 30 day increments?

I mean, really, couldn't you do just about anything for 30 days?

Let's look at 2 examples of how this would work.

Example #1 – Lose 50 Pounds

Maybe your goal is to lose 50 pounds and you're going to do it by eating healthy food with a low caloric intake and exercising for 30 minutes every day. Now, initially, you may be thrilled at the prospect of how healthy you'll feel, but then it hits you what you have just agreed to do. You begin thinking about the pain, the sacrifice, the routine, the foods that you would be giving up, etc. Your next thought is that you would have to do all of those things for a very, very long time.

Ugh!

What if:

- Instead of thinking about it being "forever", you made a 30 day daily plan? Maybe your plan is to eat salads for every meal with oil and vinegar dressing, you only snack on vegetables and give up breads and all processed foods.

- You decide that you will push yourself to exercise a minimum of 30 minutes a day…making yourself sweat and ache.

- At the end of that 30 days, you celebrate…maybe with a steak dinner and baked potato. You look at your accomplishments and adjust your daily plan for the next 30 days…eliminate what didn't seem to work, keep what did work and tweak or change what makes sense to change.

Could you make yourself stick to a plan like that for 30 days, knowing that your sacrifices will end at the end of 30 days? Most people can and do!

Example #2 – Write a Book

Maybe you have an idea for a book that you've been meaning to write. Your goal is to complete your book and get it published.

At first, the goal is exciting! You're going to finally be a published author! But, that means you have to be disciplined and actually write.

You start thinking about the writer's block, the effort, the routine, the time you would be giving up, etc. Your next thought is that you would have to do all of those things for a very, very long time.

Ugh!

What if:

- You made a plan to write every day for 1 hour.

- You tell your loved ones that your 1 hour of writing time is NOT to be interrupted.

- At the end of that 30 days, you celebrate no matter how many pages you end up having written. Maybe you go on a hike with your family or take them all to an amusement park. You look at your accomplishments and adjust your daily plan for the next 30 days…eliminate what didn't seem to work, keep what did work and tweak or change what makes sense to change.

Again, could you make yourself stick to a plan like that for 30 days? Remember, all of the sacrifices would end at the end of 30 days.

Think about it, you could give up coffee for 30 days, you could jog every day for 30 days, you could videotape yourself every day for 30 days, you could write for an hour every day for 30 days, you could, well, you get it, right?

You can do ANYTHING for 30 days!

So you make deliberate decisions (based on the goal you want to accomplish) and take determined action for 30 days. At the end of the 30 days, you ask 3 questions:

1. **In what way did the determined actions get me closer to my desired goal?**

2. **Is there something that I want to change, tweak or eliminate for the next 30 days to get myself closer to my goal?**

3. **Is there something that I want to add to my determined actions list for the next 30 days?**

The methodology of the 30-Day Reset had been proven to work over and over again. It helps you to get your brain wrapped around the idea of the change you're about to make because there is an understanding that there is an end…only 30 days away.

It also helps you to keep your emotions in check because as you feel overwhelm, you can remind yourself of how much time is left and that you can do it, you can get it done…you deserve to push through to get the results you want!

Get Results

The feedback from clients has been astounding! Not only have they gotten results, but they want to share the concept with friends. When I present the concept to audiences, I usually have people come up afterwards and tell me that they were either going to use that concept for themselves or want permission to teach it to their clients.

My clients have raved about how much more successful they have been.

Now you can too!

~~~

BOLD Factor Reflections:

Am I ready to commit myself to a 30 day plan?

What actions am I going to undertake for the next 30 days?

What am I choosing to give up over the next 30 days in order to achieve this goal?

Epilogue: Keys to Living a BOLD Life

I hope that this book has inspired you to reach great new heights and not to let the goal setting process stop you in your tracks! If that happened for you, then you're well on your way to living a life with meaning, a life full of change and growth…you're ready to start living a **BOLD** life.

There may be some of you that still need a little reassurance. You may need reassurance because you've had a difficult life or you've lived your life fearfully or you're just not sure that living boldly will make your life better.

If bold is too much, how about living powerfully and in a positive direction?

You were born full of hope and promise and I want you to grab a hold of the greatness within yourself, push the limits you've set for yourself and live your dream!

You can't tell me it's impossible. You've just read about how to accomplish impossible and read a few examples of incredible achievements. That is entirely possible for you too! To get started, you need to let go of whatever is holding you back, explore what is inside of you and believe your dreams for yourself. You are full of possibilities and potential and you need to get out of your own way.

I want to leave you with my 8 Keys to Living a BOLD Life...

Key #1
Forgive and Accept Your Past

Whatever has happened in your life has happened. You can't run from it, and as long as you continue to try, it will have a hold on you. Instead, embrace it! Acknowledge that it happened and recognize how much you have overcome in your life. You are an inspiration!

So many times, once we've reached a place that is comfortable, we stop fighting for more. We settle into a life that we understand and we don't set goals for ourselves anymore, either because we feel we don't deserve it or because we're scared.

Who says you don't deserve more? Ask yourself this question and write down the answer, "What would you do if you had the freedom to do anything in your life?"

Have you done it?

Look really hard at your answer. Envision yourself doing it. How does it make you feel inside? Now, what is keeping you from going for it? In most cases, it is your own limiting beliefs.

At one point, these beliefs may have kept you safe, but you don't need them anymore. The world is out there for you to take a hold of and make yours!

Key #2
Be Open to Accepting Help

No matter where you are in your life or where you want to go, there are people available that can help you to achieve whatever it is that you want to achieve. However, you have to be open to getting their help.

Now, help can come in many different forms. It could come in the form of a book, a religion, a retreat, a friend, a therapist or a coach, but there's someone or something out there specifically for you. You simply have to be open to recognizing it and accepting it when it comes.

Another component to accepting help is being aware that there's a difference between "doing things right" and "doing the right thing". You have a choice every single day to "do the right thing".

Sometimes, you may be tempted to be dishonest, because you "deserve" to get something. However, what you "deserve" is to treat yourself and others with respect. By not compromising your integrity, you can look at yourself in the mirror and be proud of the face that looks back at you.

Keep your options open and accept the help that is knocking on your door.

Key #3
Recognize the Strength from Your Past

---

*It's easy to forget how far you've come
when you are looking at where you want to be.*

*Take the time to write down how far you've come
and recognize just how strong you are.*
Deidre Hughey

Whatever it is that you've been through, it has made you stronger. You may ask yourself, "Well, if that's true, then why do I still feel so weak?" In answer to that, let me ask you a couple of questions in return:

Are you still focused on your past and how you've been wronged?
Do you believe that you deserve less because of your past?

If you can answer yes to either of those questions, or both, then that's why you don't feel strong. Instead, take the time to look at what you've been through and recognize how far you've come.

Here's an exercise that you can do to help you to recognize and take ownership of your personal strength. This exercise is called "Why vs. How."

In "Why vs. How", the "why" is so much more important than knowing the "how." Let me explain what I mean.

We all know "how" to do a lot of things. And don't misunderstand me, it's important to know "how" or you wouldn't get things done. However, without asking yourself "why" you're doing something, you can end up getting little accomplished for yourself.

Here's the exercise:

As you go throughout your day, ask yourself "why" you do what you do. When you get the answer, ask yourself if it's important…if it's moving you forward in your life. If it is, keep doing it.

If you realize that the task accomplishes nothing for the betterment of your life or the lives of those around you, ask yourself if this is a task that can be ignored or relegated to someone else.

In the end, you'll feel stronger, more empowered and in control of your life. You may even find that you have freed up some time that will allow you to do something special for yourself!

Key #4

Wage War Against Your Brain's Status Quo (or, Sometimes the light at the end of the tunnel is a train.)

Sad, but true! Just when you think that you're moving forward and life is going to get easier, something bad happens. Then, you're surprised, shocked or furious. After all, "Haven't I already paid my dues?"

The Bad News

After experiencing a trauma, you just want a break and it's difficult to accept reality. So, what's reality? While you may have had a tough life, life continues on and struggles will happen. Bad things happen to good people all of the time. You need to accept that life is full of adversity.

The Good News

Tough times don't last. And, with every tough time that you go through, you get tougher, more resilient and more capable. Once you accept that idea, you need to make a vow to yourself to never give up.

With every passing struggle, the struggle will become easier to handle. After a period of time, you will become a light to those around you. Someone needs you, too. And, you don't have to become a speaker or an author to have a positive effect on those around you. You just need to be aware and willing to help.

> *Go looking for conflict, and you'll find it. Go looking for people to take advantage of you, and they generally will. See the world as a dog-eat-dog place, and you'll always find a bigger dog looking at you as if you're his next meal. Go looking for the best in people, and you'll be amazed at how much talent, ingenuity, empathy, and good will you'll find. Ultimately, the world treats you more or less the way you expect to be treated.*
> **Bob Burg and John David Mann**

Key #5

Accept That There's Greatness in Your Future

While it's easy to close your mind and just exist, it's the worst thing in the world to do to yourself! There is so much to learn and embrace. Your heart and mind crave to be stretched in new directions daily and if you stop challenging yourself to learn, your heart and mind will become numb to the possibilities that surround you.

So wake up! You can find new ideas in books, religion, hobbies, sports, and by simply being with other people!

> *One of the best ways to begin to accept potential greatness is to surround yourself with friends.*
>
> *Understand them and embrace them.*
> **Deidre Hughey**

Friends make life more interesting and the struggles in life more bearable. Spend the time to make friends and value your relationships.

For 8 years, I lived near one of my dearest friends, Karen, in San Diego, CA. When my husband and I decided to move our family to the other side of the country (North Carolina), Karen and I sadly had the "woulda, shoulda, coulda" talk with each other.

Here's how it went…
"I wish we **would have** spent more time with each other."
"We **should have** made more plans."
"I **could have** moved my schedule around."

I vowed to never have that speech again and as much as I valued my relationship with Karen, I now live it. I call her frequently, and we visit as often as the distance allows. I not only show this change in my relationship with Karen, but I have made changes with new friends.

Another thought about friends…not every friend is going to fulfill all of your needs in a friend. I have several friends that I can call at 2am or could call me and we would take care of each other. However, each one is different.

I have one friend that is always encouraging and telling me how wonderful I am. She's the first person I call when I'm feeling down. I have one friend that challenges me to strive for me and push myself to only accept the best in myself. She's who I call if I'm feeling like I can't accomplish something. I have another that has a son a couple of years older than my children and gives me hope that my kids are going to turn out okay.

If I put them all in the same room, they would all get along, but they wouldn't necessarily become friends with each other. But that doesn't matter. What matters is that they all fill a part of my heart. Each of them fulfills different needs within me and I need all of them in order to continue to grow. They are instrumental to my future as I believe that I am for them.

The older you get, the more difficult it gets to make new friends, real friends, so when you do, embrace them. You'll be happier and I promise you, it will make a difference in your life and in theirs.

Key #7
Protect your personal time – don't find time, make time!

Once, I was talking with a client and I told her, "You need to make sure that you're spending at least an hour a day by yourself, for yourself."

She responded by telling me, with quite a bit of exasperation and with all sincerity, "But, where am I supposed to find the time?!"

I looked at her with a grin and said, "You'll never 'find' time for yourself; you have to 'make' time for yourself."

It sounds simple and logical. The first time someone told this to me, it was profound. I had been spending so much time doing what "needed" to get done, that I was leaving out what was most important…me. I would wager that many time, you do the same in your own life.

If you don't take care of yourself, you will run out of energy to take care of everything else in your life. In the end, it will make you sick. You need to do whatever it takes to safeguard the time that is a must ingredient for your health and sanity. I know that's easier said than done.

Make the time to take the time to be with yourself, exercise and eat right. You'll be happier and life will seem more manageable. The obstacles that come your way will be easier to overcome and you'll be able to get through your struggle with a smile on your face.

You'll love yourself for it!

Key #8
Go make a difference and be great!

I believe that we were all born to be great! I don't mean that every single one of us is born to be famous or rich. In my opinion, being great is relative to the impact that you have on people and you don't have to be Mother Theresa to have an impact.

One of the greatest people that I know is the mother of one of my childhood friends, Diane.

During a time when I stopped believing in myself and felt that no one loved me, she took me on several trips with her and her daughter. We went to amusement parks, roller skating, saw movies and stayed at the beach. I believe that her love and care for me helped me to stay alive and sane during a critical time in my life.

Years later, when I was in my mid-thirties, I visited her and through tears, told her how much her love had meant to me. She was floored. To her, she was being caring…a simple act of kindness. To me, she had been great. She had made a significant difference in my life.

Simple acts of kindness can have a greater impact than you imagine. For example, volunteering at a local organization that serves needs you care about can have a drastic impact on people's lives and help to keep you moving in a positive direction in your own life.

Here's a recap of the keys…

Key #1 – Forgive and Accept Your Past

Key #2 – Be Open to Accepting Help

Key #3 – Recognize Your Strength

Key #4 – Wage War Against Your Status Quo

Key #5 – Accept the Greatness in Your Future

Key #6 - Embrace your friends

Key #7 - Protect your personal time

Key #8 - Go make a difference and be great!

I've interviewed hundreds of men and women from all walks of life. Some are millionaire owners of corporate empires, some are doctors, psychologists, therapists and coaches, others are exploring our world while still others are happy to be homemakers.

The overriding theme is that they all found success and joy in their lives and see themselves as being successful. A success born of accepting change, letting go of the past and pushing themselves to greater heights than they could have imagined previously.

Once you move forward and become successful, it will be your turn to pay it forward. It's time to tell your story, not the story of your past, but the story of BOLD victory!

Someday, your story will inspire others to reach for their greatness.

Be BOLD, Be YOU!

Additional Quotes:

Feel the fear and do it anyway.
Susan Jeffers

An investment in knowledge always pays the best interest.
Benjamin Franklin

Don't make someone a priority that makes you an option.
Unknown

Change is inevitable. Either accept it or affect it.
Dr. Nancy Irwin

Nobody is stronger, nobody is weaker, than someone who came back. There is nothing you can do to such a person because whatever you could do is less than what has already been done to him [or her]. We have already paid the price.
Elie Wiesel (1928) Activist and American (Romanian-born) author.

Fear is misplaced energy – don't let it stop you, instead let it propel you forward to you own personal greatness!
Deidre Hughey

Mountain – get out of my way!
Dr. Glenda Clare

If you already know everything you need to know, then why aren't you where you want to be in your life RIGHT NOW?
David Neagle

Additional Quotes

Don't tell me it's impossible until after I've already done it.
Pam Lontos

Our deepest fear is not that we are inadequate. Our deepest fear is that we are powerful beyond measure. It is our light, not our darkness that most frightens us. We ask ourselves, Who am I to be brilliant, gorgeous, talented, fabulous? Actually, who are you not to be? You are a child of God. Your playing small does not serve the world. There is nothing enlightened about shrinking so that other people won't feel insecure around you. We are all meant to shine, as children do. We were born to make manifest the glory of God that is within us. It's not just in some of us; it's in everyone. And as we let our own light shine, we unconsciously give other people permission to do the same. As we are liberated from our own fear, our presence automatically liberates others.
Marianne Williamson

Face Your Fears, Live Your Dreams!
Patricia Alcivar

Follow winners and you never lose. You can be inspired by many but you have to stay true to you.
Ungenita Prevost

When you forgive, you heal your own anger and hurt and are able to let love lead again. It's like spring cleaning for your heart.
Marci Shimoff

Most of the important things in the world have been accomplished by people who have kept on trying when there seemed to be no hope at all.
Dale Carnegie

Believe in yourself – everything you need is right within you!
Dr. Karen Sherman

At the end of our lives we all ask, "Did I live? Did I love? Did I matter?"
Brendon Burchard

A ship in harbor is safe. But that is not what ships are for.
John Shedd

No one can make you feel inferior without your consent.
Eleanor Roosevelt

Courage is the most important of all the virtues, because without courage you can't practice any other virtue consistently. You can practice any virtue erratically, but nothing consistently without courage.
Maya Angelou

God grant me the serenity to accept the things I cannot change; courage to change the things I can; and wisdom to know the difference.
Reinhold Niebuhr

Formulate and stamp indelibly on your mind a mental picture of yourself as succeeding. Hold this picture tenaciously. Never permit it to fade. Your mind will seek to develop the picture…Do not build up obstacles in your imagination.
Norman Vincent Peale

Fear is not a reason to stop moving forward. In fact, sometimes when you feel fear, you are actually the closet to your greatness.
Deidre Hughey

Nothing ever changes if nothing ever changes.
Unknown

If you don't like something, change it, if you can't change it, change your attitude.
Maya Angelou
We fall down but we get up.
Unknown

If you don't try, you can't succeed; if you do try, you might surprise yourself.
Cynthia MacGregor

A thought is harmless unless we believe it. It's not our thoughts, but our attachment to our thoughts, that causes suffering. Attaching to a thought means believing that it's true, without inquiring. A belief is a thought that we've be attaching to, often for years.
Byron Katie

And, last, but certainly not least, I put one of my very favorite quotes in its entirety on the next page. This timeless and eloquent piece is by Virginia Satir. I hope you come to enjoy it as much as I do…

I am Me. In all the world, there is no one else exactly like me. Everything that comes out of me is authentically mine, because I alone chose it — I own everything about me: my body, my feelings, my mouth, my voice, all my actions, whether they be to others or myself. I own my fantasies, my dreams, my hopes, my fears. I own my triumphs and successes, all my failures and mistakes. Because I own all of me, I can become intimately acquainted with me. By so doing, I can love me and be friendly with all my parts. I know there are aspects about myself that puzzle me, and other aspects that I do not know — but as long as I am friendly and loving to myself, I can courageously and hopefully look for solutions to the puzzles and ways to find out more about me. However I look and sound, whatever I say and do, and whatever I think and feel at a given moment in time is authentically me. If later some parts of how I looked, sounded, thought, and felt turn out to be unfitting, I can discard that which is unfitting, keep the rest, and invent something new for that which I discarded. I can see, hear, feel, think, say, and do. I have the tools to survive, to be close to others, to be productive, and to make sense and order out of the world of people and things outside of me. I own me, and therefore, I can engineer me. I am me, and I am Okay.

Virginia Satir

About the Author

Deidre Hughey is the founder of 30-Day Reset, BOLD Factor Club and the author of *I AM Bound and Determined*. She is a rising star in the business and motivational training world.

Deidre is dedicated to helping people get unstuck and powerfully reset their lives. This determination comes from a personal and painful reset that she underwent herself: she survived molestation as a child, diagnosed with bipolar depression and a borderline personality disorder, suicide plans, committed to a psychiatric institution, raped twice, two abortions and drug addiction...all before the age of 20.

Deidre Hughey turned her life around 180 degrees and is now happily married, the mother of two boys, a successful business owner, professional speaker, author and previous producer and host of the popular radio talk show "3 Steps Forward".

Her speaking engagements, programs and resources have helped individuals make dramatic changes for the better in both their business and personal lives. Deidre believes, wholeheartedly, that even though life includes challenges that can slow you down, anyone can get kick their "stuck" to the curb and light a fire in their life!

Meet Deidre and receive free training at
www.DeidreHughey.com